Francis Poulenc

Sonata

for clarinet and piano

Revised edition, 2006

Edited by Millan Sachania

Chester Music

Francis Poulenc

SONATA FOR CLARINET AND PIANO

Poulenc completed the Sonata for Clarinet and Piano at Brive-Noizay late in the summer of 1962. The project had been occupying his thoughts for at least five years. He had drafted the slow movement as early as August 1959, but the demands of the *Gloria*, then in the final stages of composition, halted further progress. It was under these circumstances that Poulenc noted to R. Douglas Gibson of J. & W. Chester that the slow movement could be published as an independent 'Andantino tristamente', were he never to complete the outer movements. (The 'Andantino' later donated its 'tristamente' label to the first movement, and in the process acquired the title 'Romanza'.) Poulenc's perseverance won through, however, and in a letter dated 18 January 1963 the composer promised Gibson delivery of the fair copy within eight days. He also requested that the task of engraving the work be entrusted to 'un bon graveur assez musicien pour deviner les notes douteuses'. Twelve days later, Poulenc suddenly died. The notational ambiguities thus remained unresolved and accordingly contaminated the text of the first edition, which was published later that year.

The revised edition of 1973, prepared with the assistance of Thea King and Georgina Dobree, attempted to grapple with these textual problems. But though it made a number of useful suggestions, the scope of its amendments did not extend to improving the rough-and-ready notational style of its predecessor. In addition, a number of significant inaccuracies escaped detection.

In preparing the present edition, the direct successor to that of 1973, I have taken the opportunity to re-inspect Poulenc's fair copy. My objectives have been to reassess Poulenc's intentions, to remedy patent errors in the 1973 edition, and, wherever possible, to refine and clarify the notation. The underlying aim has been to construct a score for performing musicians along scholarly lines.

My treatment of Poulenc's accidentals has been much guided by the necessity of providing a precise but legible score. Thus the new edition encloses within square brackets accidentals that were plausibly intended by Poulenc but which are absent from the manuscript. By contrast, accidentals that are almost certainly omitted from the manuscript in error are inserted tacitly. In seeking legibility, the score both provides many cautionary accidentals not present in either Poulenc's fair copy or the 1973 text and excises Poulenc's many redundant accidentals.

The current edition also occasionally redistributes notes between the piano staves in order to enhance its visual appeal. But in this matter, as with all notational issues in the present score, the configuration is undisturbed where Poulenc's notation might have performance or other musical implications.

Perhaps the most immediately noticeable difference between the present edition and its predecessor is in the way in which they slur phrases that conclude with tied notes. The 1973 score follows Poulenc in generally ending the slur on the first of the tied notes, excluding the subsequent note or notes from the phrased unit. By contrast, the present edition consistently extends such slurs so that they incorporate the second or final tied note.

With respect to dynamic and articulation markings, parallel passages in Poulenc's manuscript do not necessarily enjoy identical levels of detail. The new edition refrains from automatically imposing consistency between such passages. In a few instances where the omission of such markings in a second or later statement of a passage is patently erroneous, it rectifies the situation tacitly. 'Corrections' more open to debate, however, appear within square brackets.

A final point: the previous edition gave certain editorial suggestions which suppressed Poulenc's own dynamic markings. The new edition restores the original indications but retains (within square brackets) some of the proposals made by its predecessor for balancing the dynamic levels of the two instruments.

MILLAN SACHANIA
Shepperton, England, 2000

Note on the 2006 edition

In preparing the 2006 edition, I have taken the opportunity to enhance the graphic presentation of the score, clarify some slurs and ties, and put right a couple of minor misprints. There are no major departures, however, from the 2000 edition.

M.S

à la mémoire d'Arthur Honegger

SONATA

for Clarinet in B♭ and Piano

FRANCIS POULENC

I

Allegro tristamente

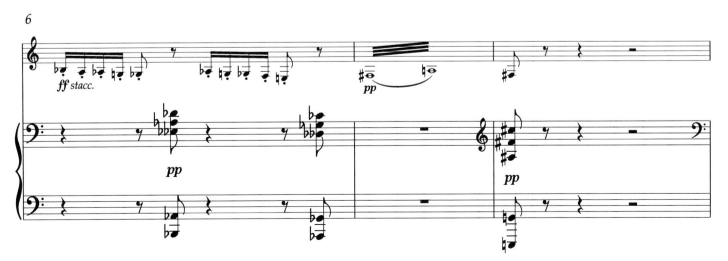

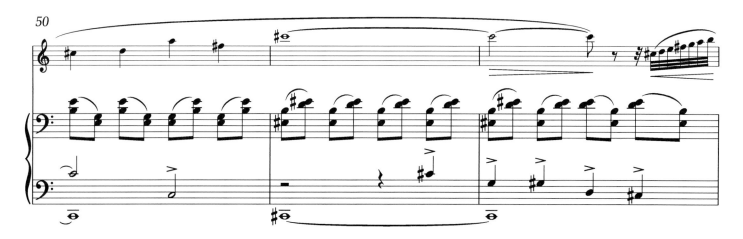

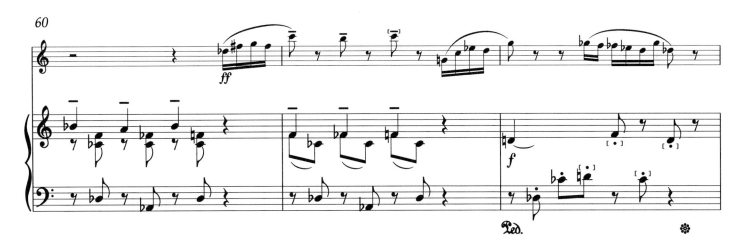

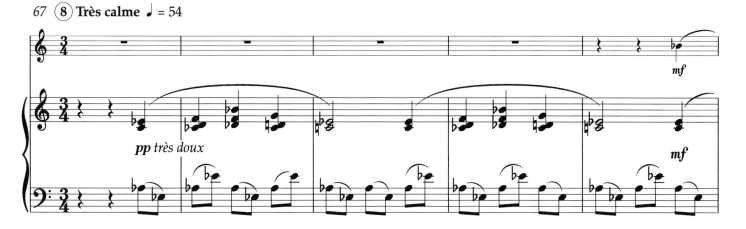

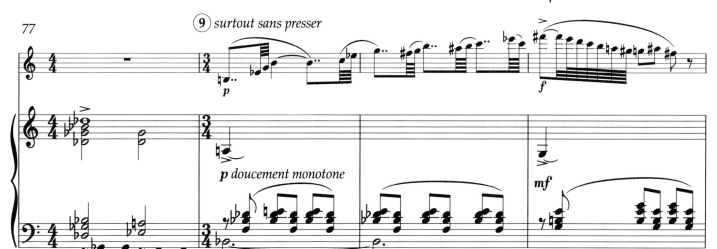

10

106 (11) **Tempo allegretto** ♩ = 136

110

114

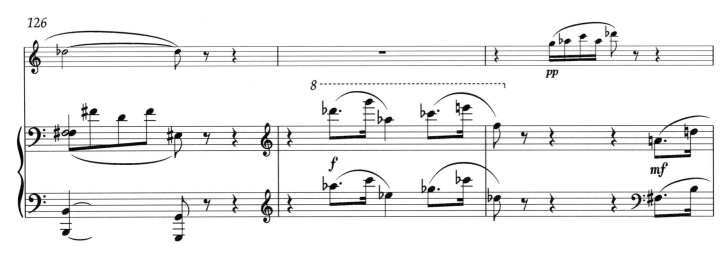

II
Romanza

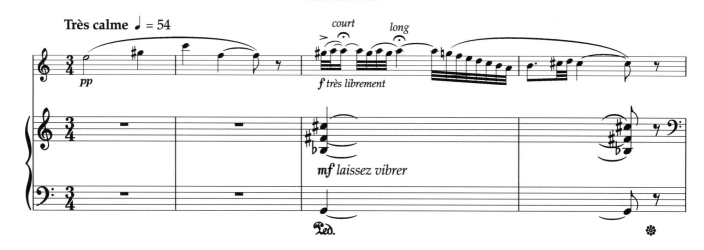

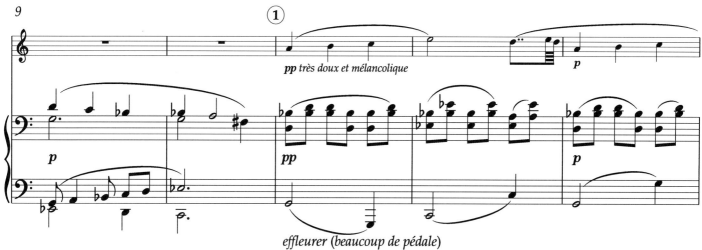

III
Allegro con fuoco

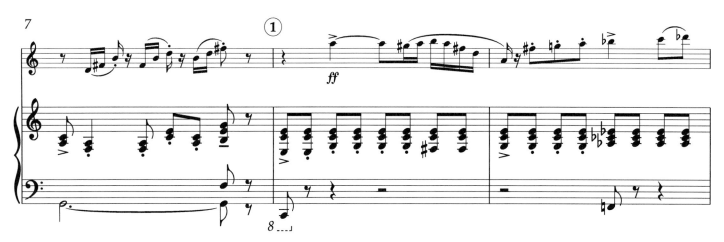

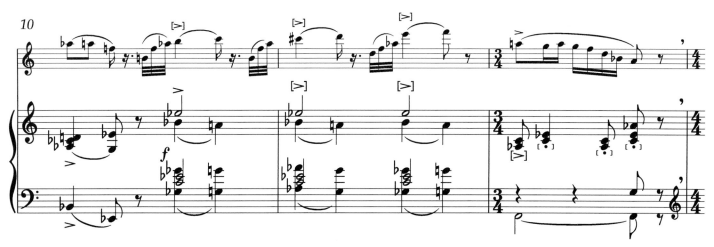

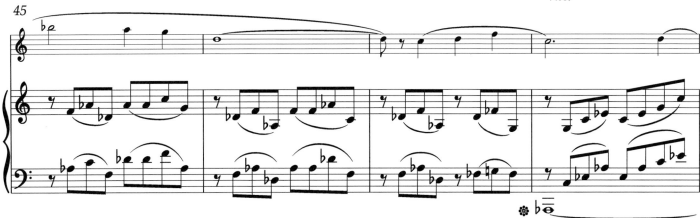

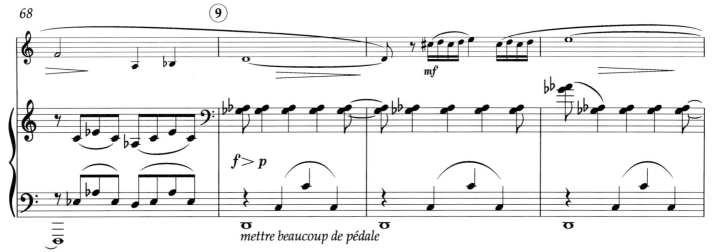

mettre beaucoup de pédale

87

91

94

98

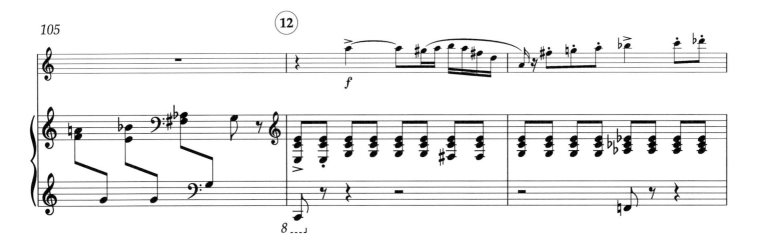

114

118

122

126

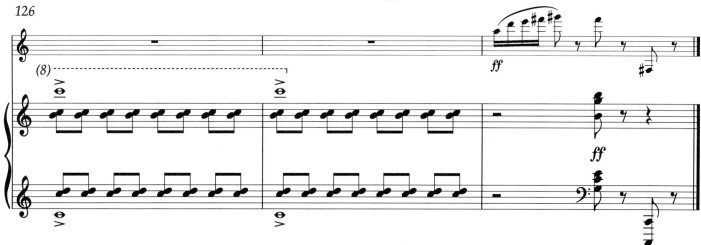

Eté, 1962